# 1 MONTH OF
# FREE
# READING

## at
## www.ForgottenBooks.com

By purchasing this book you are eligible for one month membership to ForgottenBooks.com, giving you unlimited access to our entire collection of over 1,000,000 titles via our web site and mobile apps.

To claim your free month visit:
www.forgottenbooks.com/free504431

ISBN 978-0-483-97884-3
PIBN 10504431

This book is a reproduction of an important historical work. Forgotten Books uses
state-of-the-art technology to digitally reconstruct the work, preserving the original format
whilst repairing imperfections present in the aged copy. In rare cases, an imperfection in
the original, such as a blemish or missing page, may be replicated in our edition. We do,
however, repair the vast majority of imperfections successfully; any imperfections that
remain are intentionally left to preserve the state of such historical works.

# MISCELLANEOUS POEMS

BY

## MRS. ELIZABETH ROWTON BRODIE.

INSCRIBED WITH MUCH RESPECT AND ESTEEM

TO

## LADY CROFT.

LOAN STACK

# PREFACE.

———

I publish this little volume at the request of a few friends. Written in misfortune and in a gloomy solitude, I trust it to an indulgent public.

.

**425**

# MISCELLANEOUS POEMS.

*To the Marquis of Townshend on hearing of a bereavement in his family.*

RELENTLESS fate ! to strike thee such a blow ;
Who felt for others in their hour of woe ;
Who cloth'd the naked, sooth'd the bed of pain,
And helped the homeless to a home again ;
Who saved the falling from a life of sin,
And those more shameless did to virtue win ;
Who taught the godless that there was a God,
And warn'd them of the judgments of His rod.

My lord, do thou accept my humble lay ;
'Tis all the tribute I can ever pay
For all thy kindness in my hour of need ;
But thy philanthrophy will have its meed—
Good deeds belong unto thy noble name,
Tho' thou, ere now, hast blush'd to find it fame,
Thy name will live while names of kings will die,
And thy reward is far beyond the sky !

*Complaint of an eagle in a golden cage.*

AH ! wretch undone ! O cruel fate ;
A captive ! yet in royal state,
  I gaze upon the sun.
In vain I try to fly,
In vain I beat my bars ;
  My wounded wing, my bruised head,
Bear witness to my scars,
My throne's upon the mountain top,
My mate, my children high ;
Ah ! little ever did I think my fate thus to descry !
Could nothing serve mine enemy,
  My life was in his power ;
But this—this worse than death,
  For his triumphal hour !
In calm despair I'll hear my lot,
  In scorn I'll bear my chain ;
Until my bars are rusty grown,
  Or death shall end my pain.

*Alone !*

ALONE ! alone on the world's wide sea,
  Not one to stretch a helping hand ;
My shipwrecked bark lies to the lee,
  And still afar from the wished for land.

I am alone, yet Thou art near
  To help, to save me, and defend ;
What need I fear if Thou art here ;
  The living God, my All, my Friend.

I will not mourn, I will not weep,
  I'll rest my oars upon Thy grace ;
And supplicate Thy mercies deep,
  And strive to meet Thee face to face !

## To A——

I SEE thy name amidst the names
    Of the wealthy, the careless, the gay ;
I hear of thy fame in the giddy dance,
    And yet thou know'st better than they.

Hast thou forgotten thy life was marked out,
    Not for a leader of " Ton "—
But a leader of good and noble deeds,
    And a battle that's still to be won ?

I would see thy name amidst the names
    Of the great, of the noble, the true ;
When the poor shall bless, and the good caress,
    " Well done " shall be said unto you.

Leave thon the gay and thoughtless life,
    And begin anew I pray,
Be thou foremost in the strife
    That will lead to an endless day.

And may my prayers be heard above,
    For thou, myself, and for mine ;
And so hope to meet in the world of love,
    Where only the righteous shine.

## My Cat.

WHO welcomes me when I come home
But loves me for himself alone,
And without fail expects a bone ?

                My cat !

Who spits at strangers when they share
My dinner, or takes my old arm chair,
And for whose comfort does not care

                My cat !

Who looks at me with great surprise,
And wonder in his large black eyes,
If milk's not given when I rise?

                              My cat!

Who wags his tail in great disdain,
If Tabby's called to tease the same,
When Tibby is his proper name?

                              My cat?

When I have been in bitter grief,
And tears they came, but brought relief,
Who whined and lick'd my hands and cheek?

                              My cat!

Who when I was so very ill,
My hand too weak to hold a spill,
Who took my toast and ate his fill?

                              My cat!

Who purrs away with greatest glee,
If he can jump upon my knee,
And happy only when with me?

                              My cat!

### *To my mother.*

SWEET mother! dost thou ever see
Thy unhappy child, and her deep misery?
Does thy spirit ever hover near,
To whisper comfort, or to say, " Child, do not fear "?

I often think it must be, yet, I do not know
How a blest spirit can look on human woe,
How could thy spirit soar to heaven again
And leave thy sorrowing child to earth and pain?

Sweet spirit! I hope it cannot be
That my sad lot should give a pang to thee,
I pray that my misfortunes bear not a single grain
To mar one note in thy angelic strain.

Dear mother, I can only bow and weep
And dream of thee in day-dreams and in sleep,
And as I gaze up sadly to the sky,
Methinks I see thy bright wings spread out on high.

One thing I know, sweet mother dear,
I often feel that thou art near,
And in my dreams the past comes o'er my brain,
With thee! a young and happy child again!

But oh, sweet mother, it is not so,
A crushing weight of grief I only know,
And still thy spirit seems to come and say,
" Look up my child, God is thy stay!"

*To the Rev. E——*

Ah! sadly we miss thy dear kind face,
   And thy old familiar smile,
And thy springing and elastic step,
   When we meet in the sacred aisle.

We miss thy deep and sonorous voice,
   And the " Word " that came so clear,
When to old and young thou spake
   Warnings, and comfort to cheer.

We miss thee in the morning walk,
   And in the evening stroll,
And we gaze upon thy vacant chair
   With feelings past control.

Oh! sorrow of heart we have, dear E——,
   You have left us warm hearted and true,
And will you forget us, though absent we be,
   · For others—friends that are new?

We pray thy new life may be all that thou canst wish,
   And that blessings be thine from on high,
And though we never may meet thee in this,
   We may meet in our home in the sky.

### To J——

THEY ask me why I love thee?
How can they ask me why?
Ask the flowers why they breathe perfume,
And the zephyrs why they sigh.

Ask the stars why they emit their light,
And why doth the pale moon shine?
Why doth the great sun shine so bright?
Then ask why my love is thine!

Love comes not at the human will,
But it clings to the good and the true,
And is won by kind and noble deeds,
And so my love came unto you.

Thy sympathy soothed my bleeding heart,
When bowed with grief and pain;
And the cruel deeds that caused the smart
Were covered o'er again.

God's blessings on thee, gentle one!
My gratitude and love are thine;
I'll bear thy name before the throne,
And deeds until I've done with time.

### To W. S. W.

MY dear kind friend, since last I saw
Thy gentle face and beaming eye,
Griefs have been busy in my heart,
And I have almost wished to die!

For I have lost one that I lov'd,
(And there are not many that I do)!
And though I own it to be a fault,
That fault does not extend to you.

For I do long to see thy face
　And find thy friendship still the same,
And tho' my name be soon forgot,
　I never will forget thy name!

The world's to me a fleeting shade,
　It takes my loved and best caressed.
My pets they die, my flowers they fade,
　Because I love and tend them best!

Then write to me, my "*Chere amie*,"
　And spare me the sad lot
Of grief and pain that I should feel,
　If I'm "remembered not."

*Folly and wisdom.*

Dearest Wisdom! do forgive me,
　Folly—thy adopted child,
For I've lost thy shield Ægis,
　And from thy way have been beguile.

Without thee, Mentor, I've been roaming
　Into many distant parts,
Shieldless—I met charming Cupid,
　And could not resist his darts.

For he set my heart aglowing
　With a bright and vivid flame;
Don't be angry! dread Minerva,
　You, too, might have felt the same.

Pallas! Wisdom! dear old Mentor;
　Can it be slander or is it true,
For I'm told that darling Cupid
　Only can belong to you.

Then again, "they say " that Folly
  Unto love is near of kin ;
Is it true, my great Minerva,
  And is love such a dreadful thing ?

Let me understand, dear Mentor,
  Which is false and which is true,
If love is mine without thy censure,
  All thy wisdom I leave to you.

*To seventy-four.*

THE Old Year is gone at last ;
  What is on thy wing, O New !
Take not the last remaining joys,
  I have but very few.

Be merciful to me, New Year ;
  My lot is sad and cold ;
Let me retain the few I love ;
  I lost many in the Old.

The Old Year has been a cruel foe ;
  Each hour had its knell,
And many moments seemed as years
  So bitter was its spell.

Farewell to thee, then Seventy-three,
  We shall meet on death's great shore ;
A sad farewell I bid to thee,
  Be kinder Seventy-four !

*On the death of Dr. Livingstone.*
DEDICATED TO HIS DAUGHTER.

IN Africa his toil is o'er,
  He lays him down to die,
Just on the point of coming home
  To see his own lov'd sky.

Where honours thick were awaiting him,
   And riches for the brave,
And many hearts to welcome him,
   Now—only to his grave !

But God had said, "Come up, my son !
   Thy earthly toil is o'er !
For I will be thy great reward,
   And thou shalt want no more."

So now our welcome cannot be
   What we so wished to give,
For he is gone where Jesu is—
   And where the angels live !

But Britain's sons will mourn their loss,
   And drop a heart-felt tear,
As sorrow's wreath, in gems and flowers,
   They'll place upon his bier !

---

*On the death of Mrs. Shackleton.*

DEDICATED TO THE REV. T. SHACKLETON.

A BRIDE the other day,
   Now gone to her last rest ;
So meet to leave her house of clay,
   For mansions of the blest.

Oh ! do not mourn our loss !
   Because it is her gain ;
For she will ever more be free
   From sorrow and from pain.

Thou know'st the sacred word ;
   " Leave thy fatherless to Me ; "
As yet thy children have thy love,
   But the "word" pertains to thee.

How often those we love
  Are lost by worse than death ;
By cruel acts and nameless wrongs,
  Spoken of with " bated breath."

" We'll follow her, she'll not return,"
  The Royal poet David sung ;
And heathen poets too have said,
  " Those whom God loves die young ! "

---

### To Sir Garnet Wolseley, C.B.

WE greet thee from the battle-field,
Conqueror ! brave ! and bold.
We give thee a hearty welcome
Warrior ! from the coast of gold,
We crown thee with bay and laurel ;
We lay trophies at thy feet.
Like the ancients in their peons,
Wolseley ! Hero ! we thee greet !
Our Queen thanks thee for victory,
And her people for the peace ;
And " praise and glory be to Him "
Who alone can make war cease.
" England expects men to do their duty,"
Is the motto of our land,   \
And well was it done, Sir Garnet,
By thee and thy gallant band.

---

### To the Bishop of Derry.

Return thou to dear Erin's isle,
  May angel's guard thee to the same !
There battle for the Word of Truth
  As men did of thy priestly name—

As men ef Derry years ago,
  Who, foremost, fought the Orange cause !
And put the Papists to the rout,
  And 'stablished God's and England's laws.

Farewell ! dear prelate, yet, ere long
  Return to gladden England's shore,
To cheer our own dear Eastertide
  With words of hope and joy once more.

My prayers go with thee o'er the deep :
  Meantime may heaven upon thee smile,
And welcome be to us the breeze,
  That wafts thee back to Albion's Isle.

---

*On reading that elephants drive out of the herd their aged or sick to die.*

Driven from the herd to die,
They heed not his dispairing cry,
But spurn him from them as they fly—
The aged elephant is left to die !

Wounded, weak, and wanting food,
He cannot reach a shade ;
His home is in the leafy wood,
His grave is in the glade !

And often man to fallen man
Gives scornful cruel words,
And will not lend a helping hand,
But spurns him ! as doth the herds.

And man is often cruel, too,
To the creatures God has given,
And laughs as he tortures poor dumb things,*
Nor fears the wrath of heaven !

* Cats and Dogs.

Our God doth will that man should be
Kind to brute and brother ;
For brutes they should our pity claim,
And love to one another !

Oh ! mercy show to man and beast,
My brothers to you I plead ;
And may our God His mercy show
To us all in our greatest need.

~~~~~~~~~~~~~~~~

### *Wayward child of earth to Jupiter.*

OH ! give me back my youth again ;
    Make me a happy child once more.
Free from grief and needless pain,
    To live again the rosy hours of yore.
Take back the past, and weary years ;
    Blot thou their memory from my brain ;
Melt thou my dried and frozen tears.
    Oh ! give me back my youth again !

Oh ! give me back my youth again,
    Take from me all my hours of care ;
Let mirth the golden hours proclaim,
    And love himself in chains be there.
Let me roam among the scented flowers.
    Oh ! banish from me care and pain ;
Let me live in the Elysium bowers.
    Oh ! give me back my youth again !

~~~~~~~~~~~~~~~~

### *To the Editor of the " Hereford Times."*

Well ! my friend, what shall we see
In this new change of ministry ?
Bells have sounds and many chimes,
But nothing beats our " Hereford Times."

We cannot always wear the blue ;
But to our colours we'll be true,
For " void " and "space" can have no climes,
So, can't possess a " Hereford Times."

Some people talk of this and that,
And don't know what they would be at,
They talk of politics in rhymes,
And think they beat our matchless " Times ! "

And so, my friend, we'll hope to see
The taxes down " that should not be ! "
And other things that I could " rhyme,"
When that is done I'll " chime in time ! "

I hope the Ministry will care,
And give the poor house better fare !
Then we may hope for better times,
And I will write some better " rhymes !

*To Mr. Alexis Bull on going to India.*

WE shall miss thee on the Sabbath morn
    At our solemn hour of prayer,
We shall gaze upon thy wonted place
    But we shall not find thee there.

We shall listen for thy voice to join
    The white-robed choir in praise,
But we shall miss thy gentle voice
    Whan they their voices raise.

No ! thou'st left us for a brighter sky,
    For India's distaut shore,
May honours there be waiting thee
    ( God's blessing on thee pour),

Oh ! thou wilt show to India's sons,
    How the good of England live ;
And of the good thou hast received
    Do thou most freely give !

Do teach the heathen there's a God,
    If only that little " word,"
Thou knowest not how it may grow,
    Or prosper for the Lord.

Fare thee well ! Those I love the best,
    They go—and grieve me sore,
But may we meet where " grief " is not
    And " partings " are no more !

---

### *To an absent friend.*

1ST AND 4TH VERSES FOR MUSIC.

I DO not ask thee for thy love,
    For a sad heart like mine ;
I pray thy heart may find its rest
    On some more happy shrine.
And may each dying heart be blest
    With friendship dear as thine.

I've gazed with joy upon thy face,
    It gladden'd my sad heart,
And all my heart strings kept their pace,
    For in each thou had'st a part,
Sorrow with thee could have no place,
    And memory leaves no smart.

There is but one—to Him is known
    What thou hast been to me,
And I have reaped what thou hast sown,
    And richly reaped from thee ;
And thy reward 's before the throne
    When Jesu's face thou'lt see.

Some day my grave thou may'st pass by,
    Stand by it for a time ;
If spirits hear, I'll hear thy sigh,
    Thy footsteps would wake mine ;
And flowers will spring beneath thy feet,
    And leave a hallow'd shrine.

## Changed heart.

INSCRIBED TO REV. A. ROBINSON. SET TO MUSIC BY NICHOLAS HEINS, ESQ.,
MAY, 1874.

I HEAR thou'st won another heart,
    And art gaining wealth and fame,
Thou'rt grown cold that we must part
    And another bear thy name.
Thou, too, may'st find that love not thine
    For which thou'st slighted me ;
Perchance thou'lt feel a grief like mine :
    Ah ! then thou'lt think of me.

I once was all the world to thee
    Though a thousand might be nigh,
Thy looks and smiles were all for me,
    And thy love shone in thine eye.
I soon may go to my last sleep,
    But I've forgiven thee ;
And then my wrongs will make thee weep :
    Ah ! then thou'lt think of me.

## Dreams.

INSCRIBED TO MRS. RANKIN. MUSIC BY "ERNEST," 1875.

I DARE not think upon the past,
    I hardly dare to sleep,
I dread the coming hours of night
    For dreams that make me weep.
And yet they are but happy dreams
    That have for ever fled,
Unless the dead rise from their graves,
    Or seas give up their dead.

I dream of those I've loved and lost,
    They come to me in sleep ;
I see them, hear their loving tones,
    I wake and then I weep.
I weep to find it but a dream,
    Tho' sweet the memory be,
And when I dream of those I love
    I also dream of thee !

### On the ruins of Pompeii.

Ruins of Pompeii ! 'neath the burning pave
How many found in thee a grave !
How awful was their sudden doom
Who found in thee a living tomb !
Oh ! spirits of the ancient dead
Whose souls so long from earth have fled,
How do I long to hear thy tale,
As thy deep sorrows I bewail !
I oft have wept o'er thy extinguished light,
As poring o'er the page,* at night,
I've gazed into the gloom with shudd'ring dread,
And wept o'er thee, again, fair city of the dead !
Unhappy fate ! pressed out of sight
In broad noon day of heaven's light,
While moon and stars shone on in vain,
Thou never saw'st an orb again !
Oh ! tell me thy secrets from the grave,
Was no power left in thee to save,
No god to help at thy despairing cry
But only one thing left to thee—to die ?
What speechless agony was thy wild despair,
Yet living in the hot and molten air,
In vain thou tried'st with those who did escape to fly,
Called on thy gods in vain with petrifying cry.
Oh ! heathen race ! hadest thou but learnt to pray
To " Him " who is our only stay.
The dear " Redeemer " of mankind,
Oh ! then thou wouldst that mercy find.
Not present mercy to stay descending doom,
But mercy that is found beyond the tomb,
Where death and hell have no more might,
And faith is lost in endless light !
There spirits ! of that suffering band
We hope to meet thee in that better land,
We all must meet on death's relentless shore,
Pompeiian's ! may we meet in joy to part no more !

* Bulwer's Last Days of Pompeii.

*To L——*

DEAR gentle, teasing, saucy L——,
O'er every heart thou cast'st thy spell,
Charming, joyous, always gay,
A gem that sparkles in the day.

For though a gem may shine at night,
'Tis only in a borrowed light,
This cannot then apply to you,
Though full of mischief thou art true.

May sorrow never touch the heart,
And grief from thee be far apart,
May'st thou thus always happy be,
Good and kind yet full of glee.

But grief may come to thee or thine,
For the sun does not always shine,
May God be with thee in that day,
And be thy Everlasting Stay.

But while in this life thou remain,
May'st thou gain honour, health, and fame,
And when this life thou shalt resign,
May heaven's joys be ever thine.

---

*On the opening of the Library, the gift of J. Rankin, Esq.*

SUNG BY THE SCHOOL CHILDREN, 8TH OCTOBER, 1874.

GOD bless thee ! noble Rankin !
  For thy good work begun ;
We thank thee for our libr'y
  Which cannot be " out done."
We are but little children,
  Yet we must have our say,
And greet thee with a welcome
  On this auspicious day.

And those who will come after us
  Will hand thee up to fame,
And point unto our libr'y,
  And honour Rankin's name.
Thy princely gift God prosper ;
  May heaven upon thee shine,
And when thou leavest earthly joys
  May those of heaven be thine !

### Old letters.

THOSE dear old letters ! seal them up !
  To read them I'll refrain ;
They only make my heart more sad,
  And vex my aching brain ;
For tho' I prize them more than gold,
  The sight of them brings pain.

Those dear old letters—one by one
  What joy they've brought to me,
What sorrow, grief, and what despair
  O'er hopes that ne'er could be.
The shipwreck of my dearest hopes
  Lies o'er that paper sea.

Where are the forms who wrote those lines,
  So full of love and glee ?
Ah ! some have graves in distant lands,
  And some lie in the sea.
If bitter tears could bring them back,
  They'd come to life and me.

On some old ruin have I sat,
  When in a foreign clime,
I've read those dear old letters o'er
  Under some shady lime,
Where the writers' voices seem to come
  When vesper bells did chime.

So let the dear old letters be
   Till I go to my rest ;
Then of them all a packet make
   And lay them on my breast,
Memento of those dear ones loved,
   Of earth to me the best.

---

### *To S. J. B. on her death.*

Thy birth was in the summer time,
   In the month of roses—June ;
Thy death came with the Autumn rime,
   When flowers die so soon.

I have no garland yet to fling
   Upon thy early grave ;
I've laid thee where the lark will sing,
   And by the sun-lit wave.

Daisies are growing o'er thy head,
   The violets are there,
Sweet emblems of the gentle dead,
   So young, so dear, so fair !

I weep to leave thy moss-grown bed,
   To go so far from thee ;
The dewdrops trembling o'er thy head,
   They also weep with me.

For thee this earth could have no charms,
   Thou could'st not here find rest ;
But safe in thy Redeemer's arms
   Thou art for ever blest.

Adieu ! adieu ! no earthly frown,
   No sorrow thou shalt share,
But make one jewel in his crown,
   His diadem so rare.

### On my dog Tiger.

I HAVE a dog of Scottish breed,
The gift of a true friend indeed,
And "Tiger" tho' so fierce by name,
My dog is really very tame.

I wish it to be understood,
The giver's kind and very good ;
The dog is faithful unto me,
May friends be found as true to thee.

A faithful friend is very rare
In this sad world of sin and care.
The giver then is such to me,
So love my dog, and I'll love thee.

### To my books,

COMPANIONS of my lonely hours,
How dear thou art to me,
Glad am I for all these powers,
That win my mind to thee.

I sit me in some leafy spot,
There thy pages me beguile,
While by the world I am forgot,
By thee I'm taught to smile.

In a quaint old page of history,
I learn what men can be
In some sad pathetic story,
My life I find in thee.

Some dear old friends have passed away,
And others give me pain,
While earthly joys around decay,
Thou art to me the same.

Do thou continue still my friends,
  Still fill my mind with lore,
And I will labour for these ends,
  Until I am no more.

---

### A birthday song.

HAIL! to this day! the day of birth,
  Hail! we wish thee every joy,
May'st thou live long upon the earth
  And find this life without alloy.
We wish thee health, a goodly fame;
  For thy happiness we pray,
May we with joy meet thee again,
  And welcome thee! on thy birthday!

Hail to this day! thy natal day?
  Heaven's blessings on thee pour,
May thy good star lead on the way,
  And earth's best treasure be in store.
Peace and plenty with thee reign,
  Angels 'tend thee on thy way,
May we with joy meet thee again
  And welcome thee on thy birthday.

---

### To ——

BRING me forgetfulness, and let me sleep
Far from the caves of memory deep.
I shall forget wrongs done by thee,
If forgetfulness can come to me.

Memory is dear, if it brings no regret,
But cheers the lone heart like the sweet violet;
But hearts thou hast broken, mine thou hast torn,
I fling o'er thy falsehood a mantle of scorn!

*On the death of the Rev. John Edwards, Rector of Newtown,*
*Montgomeryshire, N.W.—To his likeness.*

THY likeness hangs up on the wall,
    Thine eyes look kindly down ;
How calm and smooth thine ample brow,
    Which never bore a frown.
Methinks I hear thee gently chide
    Those who from church did stay.
How kind, persuasive were thy words
    " To come another day ! "

I miss thy letters, oh ! so much !
    For counsel which they bore,
Directing me to that blest land,
    Where thou hast gone before.
I gaze with sorrow on thy face,
    Tears blind my eyes the while ;
Alas ! those gentle lips are mute,
    Whose anger was a smile.

*Wedding Song.*

HAIL to this day ! thy wedding day !
Henceforth thou wilt have to obey ;
And tho' I wish thee every joy,
This earth may bring thee much alloy.
I wish thee health, undying love,
For God's blessing from above,
For thy happiness I pray ;
God bless thee ! on thy wedding day !
Hail to this day ! thy wedding day !
We fling the flowers across thy way—
Emblems of the joys in store,
Heaven best blessings on thee pour ;
Peace and plenty with thee reign,
And may we all meet thee again ;
Love to attend as on our way.
And ne'er regret thy wedding day !

*On the death of Captain Glynn, R.N.*

FAREWELL ! Farewell ! thy battle's o'er,
    Thy arms crossed o'er thy breast ;
What matter ? tho' we mourn thee sore,
    So thou art with the blest !

Thy ship lies still upon the sea,
    The guns they give no sound,.
The flags all hang half-mast for thee,
    With sorrow most profound.

We miss thy human sympathy,
    We mourn for thee in vain ;
Alas ! we cannot now see thee
    Nor shall ! thy like again !

*To a monkish priest,*

WHO comes now with a cloudy brow ?
I wonder what 's the matter now ?
Do children make too much a din ?
Or hast thou found another sin ?

Alas ! we find it sad as true,
Old sins remain, we don't want new !
And yet thy pride and great pretence,
Would makc us feel devoid of sense.

Thy proudful boasting of the cross
Must make us feel a painful loss
Of Him who died and did atone,
By that one act saved us alone !

We pray thee teach the light, the way,
And unto God with us to pray—
Keep us from pride in any sense,
Good Lord, give us true penitence !

Thy pride and gloom can never win
Souls to heaven, or lure from sin ;
But love and kindness is the way
And humbleness—for this we pray !

~~~~~~~~~~~~~~~~~~~~~~~~~~~~

## Gratitude.

### TO B. C. M.

I THOUGHT my sky was too serene,
   And that it could not last,
But little did I ever ween
   'Twould be so overcast.

Some clouds were floating o'er my sky
   In my bright hour of noon,
But still I deem'd no storm was nigh,
   Or 'twould not come so soon.

It fell on my defenceless head,
   And made me all forlorn.
'Twas then I wished that I was dead,
   Or never had been born.

And thou didst come and succour me
   In my most dire distress—
When kindred fail'd, no friend but thee—
   Could I do aught but bless ?

If softer shadows ever fall
   Across my evening sky.
I'll think it is thy gentle call,
   And that thy spirit's nigh.

Then none can wonder at my love
   And gratitude for thee ;
While there remains a heaven above
   I must remember thee !

## Ingratitude.

I PITY those who err and fall,
    However great their sin;
I pity those who lose their all,
    And those whose wealth they win.
But yet I scorn and pity most,
    And ever must conclude,
The man's a monster who's so lost
    To want of gratitude!

For poverty may lead to crime,
    And ignorence to sin;
We suffer for another's fault,
    For all the world's akin.
But yet I scorn that man so lost,
    And ever must conclude,
The crime to man I think the worst
    Is want of gratitude!

## Moses views the Holy Land.

HE came upon the mountain top,
    The promised land to spy;
He knew he could not enter in,
    But in that mount must die!

Oh! how he longèd for that land,
    None but himself can tell;
He knew that sin had hindered him,
    Alas! he knew too well.

For God had said unto him once,
    " I am displeased with thee;
Thou shalt not enter in that land,
    Thou only shalt it see.

"Thou with the children vexèd'st me
    In the wilderness of Zin,
When Israel strove at Meribah,
    Presumption was thy sin."

But Moses then he prayed to God—
　"I pray Thee let me go;
Oh! let me see that goodly land
　Where milk and honey flow.

"Let me go over Jordan, Lord,
　I pray Thee let me go.
To that good Mount of Lebanon,
　Where stately cedars grow.

"There is no God can do such works,
　No God exists but thee;
And if I may not enter in
　The land oh! let me see."

"Let it suffice! Thou shalt not go,"
　The Lord Almighty cried;
Then Moses meekly bowed his head,
　And laid him down and died.

The Lord Jehovah buried him,
　In Nebo for his tomb,
But no man knoweth of the place
　Until the day of doom.

Lord keep us meek as Moses was
　Before he came to Zin;
Let us not only view the land
　But let us enter in!

---

## On Zimmerman's Solitude.

Solitude is not always good,
　If it lets us have our sway;
Nor is it good to lick the dust
　In that sinful, wilful way.

For solitude is only good
　If it brings us to our God,
And gives us help to bear our cross,
　And meekly kiss the rod.

*To a young clergyman ordained priest on Trinity Sunday.*

THOU art ordained a priest this day,
  To a priesthood most divine.
One Person of the blessed Three
  Took office such as thine.

May He be here to-day
  Confirm and strengthen thee ;
And may'st thou evermore be blest
  With the presence of the Trinity !

*David and Absalom.*

OH Absalom ! my son ! my son !
  Would God I'd died for thee
Ere thou hadst done me this great wrong,
  That I from thee must flee.
My beautiful! my favourite!
  Why hast thou turned so wild?
For sharper than a serpent's tooth
  Is an ungrateful child !
I even dare not weep for thee,
  When anyone is nigh.
And though thou sought'st to take my life,
  Yet for thee I would die.
Unhappy king ! to be a king,
  And yet to be undone ;
And by a rebel put to shame,
  That rebel too, my son !
.    .    .    .    .
Yet he was slain, the beautiful!
  Who stole all hearts away.
A most disloyal, wicked son,
  Who led Israel astray.

And Arabs who pass through the dale,
   Curse him who meant to slay ;
The pillar there is Absalom's,
   And called so to this day.

*To* ——

AH ! let us go to some lone spot
   O'er which the fairies smile,
And tho' misfortune be our lot,
   Peace shall be in our isle.
For loss of fortune, I care not,
   If thou art there the while.

The flowers shall carpet at our feet
   Near mountains ever blue ;
The roses shall put forth their sweet,
   And scent us with their dew.
And there with joy we'll ever greet
   Those dear old friends so true !

*War song.*

WRITTEN ON SIR GARNET WOLSELEY.   FOR MUSIC.

MY hero is a soldier bold,
   Brave as a Spartan he ;
He went unto the coast of gold,
   To war with Ashantee.
And as he drew his sword in hand,
   The fire flashed from his eye ;
" Forward ! my men ! " was his command,
   " To conquer or to die ! "

His martial staff surround him now,
  While he looks stern and grave,
And warlike is my hero's brow,
  O'er which his plume doth wave.
Madly he urged his charger on,
  Which bore him to the fight;
Bravely he fought till he had won!
  My hero! and true knight!

*Christmas song.*

Brothers, let us sing a song,
  Let us have no folly,
For I think it to be wrong
  To be melancholy.
Let us tune the cheerful lyre,
  Let us have a frolic;
While we sit around the fire
  Don't get talking logic.

Let us all, then, young and old,
  Sing and let's be merry,
Let us fill the wassail bowl
  With some spicy sherry.
Christmas comes but once a year,
  Let us dance and let us sing,
And give the poor of our good cheer,
  And set the Christmas bells to ring!

*The maniac's request for tears.*

I've no soft tears left me to shed,
  They seem to petrify,
And my poor brain seems turned to lead
  For those sweet tears I sigh.

I used to weep another's woe
  But now can't weep my own,
For since my tears have ceased to flow
  My heart is like a stone !
Yet not from sorrow I am free,
  They tell me I am mad.
I know it not—yet it must be
  For I am always sad !
The grass would die without the dew,
  The rose would fade away,
And leaves and trees would lose their hue,
  They all would soon decay.
Oh ! for those tears for ever fled
  I've shed in childhood's hour,
O'er my birds now long since dead,
  Or o'er a broken flow'r.
Oh ! give me tears, the gentle tears,
  That fall like summer rain ;
They'll ease my heart and quell my fears ;
  Ah ! give me tears again.

### *To P. R. T.*

I FELT those tears, I knew thou wept,
  Ere thou went o'er the sea,
And often tho' in grief I slept
  I could but dream of thee ;
And all thy tokens I have kept
  Because so dear to me.

One little word from thee I crave
  " Forgiveness" let it be.
Then let me in oblivion lave
  For I deceivèd thee.
But send that word before the grave
  Shall sever thee and me !

### *To J. H.—Memoriam.*

AND thou art gone without a word
  To ease my aching heart?
I little thought, when last we met,
  We should for ever part.
What agony came over me
  When told that thou wert dead,
Life seemed then so valueless,
  With heart and brain like lead.
I know not where they've laid thy head,
  That head so dear to me,
I've sought in vain to find thy grave,
  And compassed land and sea !
Does thy dear spirit ever see
  Thy friend thou'st left behind?
Ah ! then thou'lt see her agony
  For having been unkind.
Oh ! may we meet in that dear land
  Where partings are unknown,
And we shall never part again
  When once before the Throne !

### *To M——*

BRING to me those promised flowers,
  If I am not forgot !
The snowdrop, daisy, daffodil,
  And the blue " forget-me-not."
Cull for me the sweet wall-flower,
  The violet so blue ;
And pansy, rose, jesamine white
  Will tell me thou art true.
Bring with thee some heliotrope,
  A spray from a pear tree ;
Myrtle, and periwinkle white
  Will tell my love for thee !

And don't forget to bring some ferns,
  With ivy evergreen,
Lauristinus, Christmas rose,
  And mistletoe, I ween !

*On visiting Uttoxeter in 1876, and missing Dr. Fletcher.*

I miss'd a face I used to see,
  A voice I used to hear ;
Who tended those I lov'd and lost,
  To whom they were so dear.

He came unto my dying ones,
  And to the newly-born,
And lingered by their weary couch,
  From night to early morn.

What is the name of this good man,
  Whom all hold up to fame ?
The man is a philanthropist,
  And " Fletcher" is his name !

*Scraps.*

Ah ! gather flowers while you may,
  Give way not to dispair,
The life of man is but a span,
  And full of toil and care.

We all should cull the little joy
  That springs up in our way,
For pleasures they are very coy
  And don't come every day.

Then grasp the nettle very light,
  And grasp the samè your wrong ;
Might is not alway in the right,
  The victor's often wrong !

### *The dark spirit of Saul.*

THE spirit of Saul is o'er me now,
  Is there nothing to charm it away?
Has David's bright spirit gone with the light
  As daylight goes down with the day?
Oh! send for a harp, and the harper recall,
  And sing me of heavenly things,
For my javelin now has entered the wall
  How fearful discordant it rings.
There! there! I am soothed and at peace,
  The evil has gone from me now;
On! on! for the kingdom of grace,
  And stay not my hand from the plough!

### *To V——*

So many weeks have passed away
  And yet thou hast not come,
Nor written as thou promis'dst me,
  What is it I have done?
Thou canst not make a prisoner
  On any slight pretence,
Nor can a prisoner be arraigned
  Without stating his offence.
It is not right to use me thus,
  'Tis right my fault to tell;
Nor will I own to very much
  But loving thee too well!
And is our friendship to end thus
  To add to my despair?
Is all the fruit that I may eat
  That of the dead sea air?
Oh! write to me my dearest V——,
  And let me see thy face,
Or send thy "carte" that I may feel
  No longer in disgrace!

## *Idols.*

Ah ! never make an idol girls
  Of any living thing,
For idols can so serpent like
  Give you a deadly sting
You cannot trust unto a man
  Whom you have petted much,
But you will find him to his shame
  To prove a broken crutch !

And children are most ungrateful
  If they are petted too,
In fact with all your idols
  You'll find enough to do,
For animals can faithful be
  If they can have their fling,
But idols can so serpent like
  Give you a deadly sting !

## *To Sissy.*

Go tell the flowers I love thee,
  Whisper it to the bee ;
Queen of the lovely rosebuds,
  And sweeter far to me !

May thy lot in life be happy,
  Free from sin and care ;
Still keep thy purity of heart,
  Queen ! of rosebuds fair.

Partings come often in this world of woe,
  Thou leav'st me, or I from thee must go ;
"Good-bye !" to me has a bitter knell !
  Yet it must be ! Farewell ! Farewell !

Jesu! unto Thee I fly,
Hear me when to Thee I cry;
Hide me for the storm is nigh,
Do Thou receive my dying sigh.
Jesu! Master! ever blest,
Take me to eternal rest,
In righteousness let me be drest,
Receive me to Thy loving breast.
Jesu! everlasting stay,
Help me when to Thee I pray,
Show Thou me the narrow way.
Hold me! then I shall not stray!
Jesu! forgive the sinful past,
From Thee let me not be cast,
Save me from the tempter's blast,
Oh! receive me home at last!
Calm, oh calm, my sad fears,
Save me from the tempter's leers,
Take me home, for time it wears!
Safe with Thee from this earth's snares.

## To Louisè.

Sweet one! my muse can never pen
    All it thinks of thee!
Nor do my heartstring's music sing,
    But when thy face I see.
How kindly thou hast tended me,
    In sickness and in woe;
Thy nursing and thy gentleness
    None but myself can know.
Forgive me if I ever set
    A pattern thou should'st not take;
And do thou pray for better light,
    Before it be too late.

Forgive me for my hasty speech,
   And for each angry word ;
The bitterness I know too well—
   'Tis sharper than a sword.

Would God that I had done the right
   That I was taught when young.
And maybe 'tis the oldest song,
   Which all the world have sung ;

Oh ! do not sin as I have sinned,
   For pride's a dreadful sin ;
Scorn not the ills that I have scorned,
   But take it as from Him.

Do thou all God's commandments keep,
   Oh ! try to win a crown !
Oh ! don't thou lose eternity
   Because the world may frown !

When God He doth His jewels count,
   I pray that thou'lt make one ;
And may He hear my earnest prayer,
   For Jesu Christ His Son !

1857.

*On the death of Captain Arthur Brisco, who died on a tour*

*in America.*

My beautiful ! my brave ! sleep on
   In thy grave in the far west ;
Thy worldly strife and battles o'er,
   Warrior ! sleep on and rest ;
They've laid thee in a soldier's grave
   With thy trappings on thy breast !

No more thou'lt hear the bugle sound
　Or "rat tat tat" of the drum ;
Nor the note of clarion shrill
　Nor sound of the morning bomb ;
No more thou'lt hear the cannonade
　For with battles thou hast done !

In spirit I kneel by thy grave
　All but the birds are still ;
One gives a cry—the Priarie bird—
　With a plaintive " whip-poor-will ;
She fills the redman's hunting grounds
　And solitude with her " twill."

My beautiful ! my brave ! sleep on !
　Rest ! in a warrior's grave ;
Though boundless is that western land
　O'er it my tears I lave ;
Yet I still live ! and thou art gone !
　My warrior dear and brave !

### Foul and fair.

FOR a time I'm a spirit living in air,
I will write you all I see from there ;
Let the record be " foul and fair !"

I wing my way through a prison with dread :
A woman is weeping with a bowed head,
She is sent to prison for stealing bread ;
Yet her children by her have to be fed,
For her husband from her for years has fled,
And she knows not if he be living or dead.
She tried hard to do right, but she fell in despair,
And no wonder ! so I write this up " fair !"

I wing on my way in the silent night,
Her husband I found in a very sad plight ;
He was living in plenty, but riotous sin,
No shame or remorse without or within.
    As I'm a spirit living in air,
    I write this as "foul," and not as "fair."

I'm again on the wing in the night's kind shade,
And find a man of wealth and grade,
And a lonely woman, deserted, betrayed,
To whom is born, without a name,
A child to inherit its parent's shame ;
(Tho' the woman, of course, is only to blame) !
For the world gives the man honour and fame.
My soul burns with anger against the man,
For the woman now does the worst she can.
    As I'm a spirit living in air,
    I write this as "foul," and not as " fair."

I waft my soft wings to a different sight,
A poor woman is dying in the silent night ;
A neighbour is with her, no fire or light,
But she does what she can for her friend with her mite.
Hunger is there in both of the homes,
They cannot make bread from stocks or from stones,
So she runs for her crust from her cupboard so bare
For her dying friend—but she is not there—
No ! she died while her friend ran home in despair,
But she is now safe from want and from care
She has gone where the hungry need no fare.
    As I'm a spirit living in air
    I write this deed as fair most " fair."

---

### To his Royal Highness the Prince of Wales.

WE welcome thee from India
    Dear Prince as brave as fair,
Whilst thou wert in that distant land
    Our hearts were full of care.

We felt with those thou left behind
   Thy mother and thy wife,
And greet thee with the Danish pearl
   Of which thou art the life.

We read with wonder thy dread sport
   In dangers not a few,
Thy deadly conflict with wild beasts
   And tigers which thou slew.

India can boast of priceless gems
   And jewels rich and rare,
But the fairest in her diadem
   Is our dear England's heir!

And kingly gifts they gave to thee
   Worth more than weight in gold,
And truer hearts they cannot give
   Than those of English mould.

We feared thy safety in that land
   Thy perils o'er the main,
And we rejoice with loyal hearts
   To see thee home again.

Dear Prince! accept our welcome then
   Tho' humble it may be,
It is the language of our hearts
   That pray for thine and thee!

---

DEAR little Nellie—the joy of my heart,
The dearest and best, they always depart;
But wisely ordained, if it always be so,
That the meeting again put our hearts in a glow.

Alas! it is lonely to be without thee,
And "Robin" and "Evy" I can't always see;
But oh! for the days that to me were so bright,
When the sight of those faces gave me such delight!

*Joseph and his brethren.*

THERE stood before an ancient king
 A youth of royal mien,
From prison brought for an offence
 Of which he did not dream.
For envy, sold by brethren,
 Because they hate him sore ;
But mourned much by Israel,
 For Joseph he lov'd more.
But God had sent him to that land,
 To save them all alive ;
He was made the governor there,
 And what he did—did thrive.
When Jacob saw that there was corn
 In Egypt he could buy,
He said unto his sons " Go down
 And get some ere we die."
And Joseph knew his brethren,
 But him they had forgot ;
And spoke roughly unto them,
 When told that " One was not."
And made them all his prisoners,
 And said " Ye've come to spy !
But bring ye Benjamin unto me,
 And so ye shall not die."
" Verily we most guilty are,
 Concerning our brother ;
When he besought we would not hear,
 One spake to the other."
Then Joseph turn'd awry and wept,
 And though he understood,
They knew it not but what he did
 Was all done for their good.
And Jacob said, when told these things,
 " Ye have bereaved me !
Joseph is not—and Benjamin
 Shall not go down with thee."

But when they had ate up the corn,
  Again they saw that land ;
With double money in their sacks,
  And presents in their hand.
And Joseph asked if all were well ?
  Of the old man's welfare ?
Then sought his chamber, where he wept,
  Then did there dinner share.
He tried to stay his brethen,
  Put money in their corn ;
And had a cup put in a sack—
  In that of the youngest born.
The men were overtaken then,
  The sacks brought to the ground ;
" A bondsman he must ever be
  With whom the cup was found."
The cup was found with Benjamin,
  Then were they full of care ;
And bowed them down at Joseph's feet,
  Besought him in despair.
And told him of their father's grief,
  And Judah did draw nigh—
" I pray let me thy servant be,
  For fear our father die."
Then Joseph could no more refrain
  And told them to " come near,"
And wept and kissed his brethren
  " I'm Joseph, do not fear."
He sent his father many things
  To them he gave some more,
And commanded all to come to him
  To share with him his store.
When Jacob heard the words that came
  To them he did reply,
" Joseph my son is yet alive,
  I'll see him ere I die."
And Jacob did his dear son meet
  Stolen from him when a child,
And Joseph kissed his father much
  And wept o'er him a while.

When Joseph died a king arose
Who did not Joseph know,
Then Israel suffered many things
And went through scenes of woe.

*On seeing a pet bird die who had been shot.*

POOR darling bird! no more thou'lt fly,
Or feed among the barley rye,
Or sing thou unto me.
No, little bird! thy life is done,
For cruel man with cruel gun
Leaves me to weep for thee!

Thy broken wing, and glazing eye,
Tells me my darling thou must die!
And my heart bleeds with thee.
Could I have stay'd the heartless deed,
Or soothed thee in thine utmost need,
I should not mourn for thee!

*On the death of Mrs. Corbett.*

DRAW down the blind for our dear dead
She needs no light from the sun;
Her spirit from the earth has fled,
And her sunlight has begun.
'Tis we who mourn, who need the light
While unto the earth we cling;
Until the Righteous Sun with might
Brings healing in His wing.
We've laid her in her lonely bed
With flowers upon her breast;
Her body's with the sacred dead,
Her soul is with the blest.

Lightning Source UK Ltd.
Milton Keynes UK
UKHW012011021218
333216UK00014B/2543/P